PROFITABLE PROBLEM-SOLVING WORKBOOK

15 important steps to make money from creating solutions via critical thinking, brainstorming and mindstorming.

IREDAFENEVESHO OWOLABI

IREDAFENEVESHO OWOLABI

Some other Fast-selling Books By the author are:

- Kingdom Verities
- How to Enjoy Kingdom Currency (Vol. 1)
- How to Maximize Kingdom Currency (Vol. 2)
- Kingdom Currency for Students, Graduates and Businessmen (Vol. 3)
- Unlocking Your Kingdom Creativity
- 4-D THINKING
- Why you should Write a Book
- How to Turn your Knowledge to Money
- How to Turn Wisdom Currency to Money
- How to Make Millions as an Author-preneur
- 18 Steps to Write a Book Successfully
- How to Launch, Sell and Market your Books Profitably
- How to Successfully Self-Publish Your Books
- 15 Hot Markets Where You Can Easily Sell Your Books
- Creativity Accelerator
- Idea to Profitable Creation

TABLE OF CONTENT

IREDAFENEVESHO OWOLABI

INTRODUCTION

Are you interested in problem solving? Do you have a knack for generating ideas in order to meet pressing needs and painful problems?

Do you know that you possess in you, the painkiller to the ache of someone out there who is hurting?

Do you know that problem-solving is a skillset that can be learned and honed?

Problem-solving, creativity and critical thinking skills have become the most sought-after skills across industries and geographies.

It is therefore imperative that you begin to hone that inherent ability of yours in a profitable way by solving problems in your place of work, industry, home and nation at large.

This workbook is designed to help you fly your thoughts into the realm of 4th Dimensional Thinking so that you can become aware that you carry solutions to the problems of this generation. You will not stop there but will be guided by this material to go ahead, create the solution and monetize your solution easily and profitably.

Are you willing to create a good side income that fetches you not just more money but extra satisfaction with things that come naturally to you?

Do you want to create a business that works for you rather than the other way round? Every problem is a business.

6

Money changes hands when you proffer solutions but not everyone knows how to bring this solution out from within.

That is why you need this workbook!

I have prepared it in a manner that would help you engage in some critical-thinking, brainstorming and mindstorming.

If you take it seriously, the results would astound you.

For better results, I advise that you take time to go through all the sections. Any part you cannot give answers to, do some more research and consult some other of my Creativity and 4-D Thinking books in the series in order to make the most of this guidebook. So, grab a pen and get to work as you hone your problem-solving skills.

SECTION I

PAIN POINTS

- What problem(s) is your existence supposed to solve in real and practical terms? (Avoid ambiguous answers, the simpler the better!)

- What problem(s) is your business, craft or career supposed to solve in real and practical terms? (Avoid ambiguous answers, the simpler the better!)

- What are the major concerns or complaints that customers (clients or bosses) in your industry have today?

- What are the unique problems you have identified in these different areas which should be tackled by somebody?

Your Workplace	
Your Business	

IREDAFENEVESHO OWOLABI

Your Industry	
Your Nation	

Other	

SECTION II

REMEDY

- Which of these problems do you think you can remedy or should solve right now, from where you are, with what you have?

Your Workplace	
Your Business	

IREDAFENEVESHO OWOLABI

Your Industry	

Your Nation	
Other	

- Why do you think you should provide a solution to that problem? I mean, there are probably a dozen others who could do this, why do you think you can proffer a remedy?

- Have any previous solution or remedy been provided before now? If yes, what are they?

Your Workplace	

Your Business	

Your Industry	
Your Nation	

Other	

- Why do you think the previous solutions require a change for something new?

- If you have no limitation whatsoever, if you had all the finances, resources, personnel, etc, what would you do to solve these problems?

Your Workplace	

Your Business	
Your Industry	

Your Nation	

Other	

SECTION III

OPPORTUNITY

- What are your plans to solve these problems right now?
  (E.g. Ideas, discoveries, research, collaborations, write a book, propositions, going digital, developing a tech, automating, pricing systems, policies, etc) Be specific. For example, I will schedule a meeting with Mr. XYZ this week. Or I will research on XYZ today, or I will take XYZ approach from no henceforth, etc. Do not procrastinate the action, pick up that phone and make the calls or do the research now!

Your Workplace	

IREDAFENEVESHO OWOLABI

Your Business	
Your Industry	

Your Nation	

Other	

- With your present finance, resource, personnel, etc, can you begin to execute these opportunities and prospects?

a. If NO, why not?

SECTION IV

BENEFITS

- If your answer to the previous question is YES, are there potentials for profit or benefit in your solutions and execution plans? If yes, what are your parameters for judgment?

Your Workplace	

Your Business	
Your Industry	

Your Nation	

Other	

- How do you intend to harness these prospects?

- If No, remember that every problem is a business depending on how it is solved. There may be something you are not getting right and that is why there seems to be no monetary value attached to your solutions. Get a mentor to help you fix that!

- Who are the people who will benefit from your solutions? (Write out specifically the people who you already sell to and who you intend to sell your solutions to e.g. students, couples, bankers, mums, young professionals, etc. BE SPECIFIC!)

- Do the people listed above really need the solutions/remedy you offer?
  a. Why would they need your solutions and why would they pay for it?

b. In what specific and obvious way does
   your remedy help make their life better?

SECTION V

YOUR LEVERAGE

- Everyone has something in his immediate possession or environment that can be used as leverage. Leverage helps you achieve more with less. What kind of leverage do you possess? (Experience, skill, capacity, language, resources, network, etc).

IREDAFENEVESHO OWOLABI

- Are you satisfied with your leverage? What are you doing to gain a greater advantage in your field in other to position you as the go-to-person?

SECTION VI

IREDAFENEVESHO OWOLABI

EVOLVE

- What are the conventional ways of doing things (e.g. marketing, sales, customer service, recruitment, promotion, production, processing, etc) in your industry?

Your Workplace	

Your Business	
Your Industry	

Your Nation	

Other	

- Which of these methods are working and which ones are not working? Which ones are becoming obsolete? And which ones can be improved upon even if it's already working? (It is time to evolve through reinvention!)

Your Workplace	

Your Business	
Your Industry	

Your Nation	

Other	

- What are the methods that you need to reinvent in order to meet up or surpass the changing trend of your market, industry or the world?

Your Workplace	
Your Business	

Your Industry	

Your Nation	
Other	

SECTION VII

IREDAFENEVESHO OWOLABI

MULTIPLY

- What state of the art ideas have you conceived that will help you reach more people in your nation, business or industry?

- What plans do you have to reach more people with your solutions?

- (When Henry Ford made mass production possible, he created another problem that also needed a solution. Mass need for workers, mass need for petroleum, he factored some of these solutions in his plans. You should think in the same direction!) What problems will be created when you multiply and how can you also tackle such problems and their allies?

SECTION VIII

IREDAFENEVESHO OWOLABI

STRATEGY

- What problem(s) is your existence supposed to solve in real and practical terms? (Avoid ambiguous answers, the simpler the better!)

- What problem(s) is your business, craft or career supposed to solve in real and practical terms? (Avoid ambiguous answers, the simpler the better!)

- What are the major concerns or complaints that customers (clients or bosses) in your industry have today?

- What are the unique problems you have identified in these different areas which should be tackled by somebody?

Your Workplace	
Your Business	
Your Nation	

Other	

SECTION IX

OVERCOMPENSATE

- Which of these problems do you think you can remedy or should solve right now, from where you are, with what you have?

Your Workplace	
Your Business	

Your Industry	
Your Nation	
Other	

- Why do you think you should provide a solution to that problem? I mean, there are problem a dozen others who could do this, why do you think you can proffer a remedy?

IREDAFENEVESHO OWOLABI

- Have any previous solution or remedy been provided before now? If yes, what are they?

Your Workplace	
Your Business	

Your Industry	
Your Nation	
Other	

<table>
<tr><td></td><td></td></tr>
<tr><td></td><td></td></tr>
<tr><td></td><td></td></tr>
<tr><td></td><td></td></tr>
<tr><td></td><td></td></tr>
<tr><td></td><td></td></tr>
</table>

- Why do you think the previous solutions require a change for something new?

<table>
<tr><td></td></tr>
<tr><td></td></tr>
<tr><td></td></tr>
<tr><td></td></tr>
<tr><td></td></tr>
<tr><td></td></tr>
<tr><td></td></tr>
<tr><td></td></tr>
<tr><td></td></tr>
</table>

| |
| |
| |
| |
| |
| |
| |
| |
| |
| |
| |

- If you have no limitation whatsoever, if you had all the finances, resources, personnel, etc, what would you do to solve these problems?

| Your Workplace | |
| | |

Your Business	
Your Industry	

Your Nation	
Other	

SECTION X

LIMITING FACTORS

- What are your plans to solve these problems right now?

  (E.g. Ideas, discoveries, research, collaborations, write a book, propositions, going digital, developing a tech, automating, pricing systems, policies, etc) Be specific. For example, I will consult with Mr. XYZ this week, month or year. Or I will research on XYZ today, or I will take XYZ approach from now henceforth, etc. Do not procrastinate the action, pick up that phone and make the calls or do the research now!

Your Workplace	

Your Business	
Your Industry	

Your Nation	
Other	

a. With your present finance, resource, personnel, etc, can you begin to execute these opportunities and prospects?

b. If NO, why not?

c. What have you done and what are you actively doing to avoid the hindrances or sort them out?

IREDAFENEVESHO OWOLABI

SECTION XI

VALUE

- If your answer to the question a in Section X is YES, are there potentials for profit or benefit in your solutions and execution plans? If yes, what are your parameters for judgment?

Your Workplace	
Your Business	

IREDAFENEVESHO OWOLABI

Your Industry	
Your Nation	

Other	

- How do you intend harnessing these prospects?

- If No, remember that every problem is a business depending on how it is solved. There may be something you are not getting right and that is why there seems to be no monetary value attached to your solutions. Get a mentor to help you fix that!

- Who are the people who will benefit from your solutions? (Write out specifically the people who you already sell to and who you intend to sell your solutions to e.g. students, couples, bankers, mums, young professionals, etc. BE SPECIFIC!)

IREDAFENEVESHO OWOLABI

- Do the people listed above really need the solutions/remedy you offer?
b. Why would they need your solutions and why would they pay for it?

c. In what specific and obvious way does your
    remedy help make their life better?

IREDAFENEVESHO OWOLABI

SECTION XII

NURTURE

- Everyone has something in his immediate possession or environment that can be used as solution to problems is harnessed, processed and nurtured. What kind of leverage do you possess? (Experience, product, service, skill, capacity, language, resources, network, etc). What have you done to process this resource until it is ready to meet a high value need? How long have you been at it?

- What more do you intend to do to process this valuable resource, skill or commodity? What are you doing to gain a greater advantage in your field in order to position you as the go-to-person? Be very detailed as much as possible.

IREDAFENEVESHO OWOLABI

SECTION XIII

INITIATIVE

- **An initiative is also known as a new development; a fresh approach to something; a new way of dealing with a problem. It can be seen as the ability to act first or on one's own. When you unlock your creativity, you become an initiator.**

- What are the conventional ways of doing things (e.g. marketing, sales, customer service, recruitment, promotion, production, processing, etc.) in your industry? And what initiative are you taking to pioneer a change or make a difference?

Your Workplace	

Your Business	
Your Industry	

Your Nation	
Other	

- Packaging matters! How do you plan to package this solution that you have developed into sellable and revenue generating equivalents?

Your Workplace	
Your Business	

Your Industry	
Your Nation	
Other	

- What are the basic tools and necessities that you need to acquire or utilize in order to meet up or surpass the changing trend of your market, industry or the world?

Your Workplace	

Your Business	
Your Industry	
Your Nation	

Other	

IREDAFENEVESHO OWOLABI

SECTION XIV

GENERATE

- **Think of the different ways you can generate revenue through your solutions. These different ways represent your merchandise. The more merchandise you can generate, the more profitable you become as a problem solver.**

- What are the different products and services you can generate from your existing product, service, skill, resource, property, business, and so on?

| |
| |
| |
| |
| |
| |
| |

<table>
<tr><td></td></tr>
<tr><td></td></tr>
<tr><td></td></tr>
<tr><td></td></tr>
<tr><td></td></tr>
</table>

- How much do you intend to sell them? How much does a similar produce or service go for?

<table>
<tr><td></td></tr>
<tr><td></td></tr>
<tr><td></td></tr>
<tr><td></td></tr>
<tr><td></td></tr>
<tr><td></td></tr>
<tr><td></td></tr>
<tr><td></td></tr>
<tr><td></td></tr>
<tr><td></td></tr>
</table>

- What is your unique selling point?

IREDAFENEVESHO OWOLABI

SECTION XV

MINE YOUR MIND

- The most valuable mine on earth is the mine of the mind. What state of the art ideas have you conceived that will favour a major shift in your nation, business or industry?

- What efforts are you making to research for novel solutions?

```
┌──────────────────────────────────────────┐
│                                            │
└──────────────────────────────────────────┘
```

- (When Henry Ford made mass production possible, he created another problem that also needed a solution. Mass need for workers, mass need for petroleum, he factored some of these solutions in his plans. You should think in the same direction!) What problems have your solutions created and how can you also tackle such problems and their allies?

```
┌──────────────────────────────────────────┐
│                                            │
├──────────────────────────────────────────┤
│                                            │
├──────────────────────────────────────────┤
│                                            │
├──────────────────────────────────────────┤
│                                            │
├──────────────────────────────────────────┤
│                                            │
├──────────────────────────────────────────┤
│                                            │
├──────────────────────────────────────────┤
│                                            │
├──────────────────────────────────────────┤
│                                            │
├──────────────────────────────────────────┤
│                                            │
└──────────────────────────────────────────┘
```

IREDAFENEVESHO OWOLABI

IREDAFENEVESHO OWOLABI

PLEDGE/COMMITMENT

I _____ PLEDGE
TO TAKE ACTION IN ORDER TO RELEASE THE
PROBLEM SOLVER IN ME FOR THE BENEFIT
OF THOSE WHOSE PROBLEMS I WAS
ORDAINED TO SOLVE.

Signed _____

Date _____

Additional Notes

....

....

....

....

....

....

....

....

....

....

....

....

....

....

....

....

....

IREDAFENEVESHO OWOLABI

....

....

....

....

....

....

....

....

....

....

....

....

....

....

....

....

....

IREDAFENEVESHO OWOLABI

....

....

....

....

....

....

....

....

....

....

....

....

....

....

....

....

....

IREDAFENEVESHO OWOLABI

....

....

....

....

....

....

....

....

....

....

....

....

....

....

....

....

....

IREDAFENEVESHO OWOLABI

....

....

....

....

....

....

....

....

....

....

....

....

....

....

....

....

....

....

IREDAFENEVESHO OWOLABI

ABOUT THE AUTHOR

Iredafenevesho Owolabi (Iredafe or Dafe for short) is a Creativity Coach with the goal of helping individuals and organizations move from idea to profitable creations. He redefines public speaking with cutting-edge kingdom insights. He is happily married to the love of his life.

He facilitates seminars, training, workshops and conferences for schools, banks, businesses, churches, and organizations around the world.

His books are being read in different parts of the world with countless testimonials of their impact. He mentors several aspiring authors to success via coaching calls and his book titled "How to Make Millions as An Author-preneur" is a must-have for all authors and aspiring author-preneurs who intend to master the business of their writing gift.

He speaks to different professionals and seminars via his seminars focusing on topics like Authorpreneurship, Creativity Accelerator, 4-D Thinking, Unlocking Potential, Reinvention, Kingdom etc.

To invite him or schedule him for a presentation, send him a mail via iredafeowolabi@gmail.com.

For tips and information on how to publish and market your books successfully and effectively, get "How to Make

Millions as An Authorpreneur" and other books by Iredafenevesho Owolabi.

His Books include:

- Kingdom Verities
- How to Enjoy Kingdom Currency (Vol. 1)
- How to Maximize Kingdom Currency (Vol. 2)
- Kingdom Currency for Students, Graduates and Businessmen (Vol. 3)
- Kingdom Money
- Unlocking Your Kingdom Creativity
- 4-D THINKING
- Why you should Write a Book
- How to Turn your Knowledge to Money
- How to Turn Wisdom Currency to Money'
- How to Make Millions as an Author-preneur
- 18 Steps to Writing a Book Successfully
- How to Launch, Sell and Market your Books Profitably
- How To Self-Publish Your Books
- Creativity Accelerator

And lots more.

They are all available on Amazon in different formats.

www.ingramcontent.com/pod-product-compliance
Lightning Source LLC
Chambersburg PA
CBHW030654220526
45463CB00005B/1767